HOGANS : Navajo Houses & House Songs

HOGANS

NAVAJO HOUSES & HOUSE SONGS

House poems from Navajo ritual
translated and arranged by DAVID P. McALLESTER

Photographs of Navajo houses
by SUSAN W. McALLESTER

WESLEYAN UNIVERSITY PRESS
Middletown, Connecticut

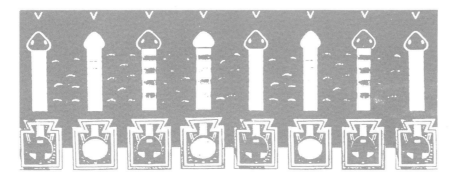

The publisher gratefully acknowledges the support of the publication of this book by the National Endowment for the Arts.

Passages from *Blessingway*, by Leland C. Wyman, and *Navajo Blessingway Singer*, by Charlotte J. Frisbie and David P. McAllester, copyright © 1970 and 1978 respectively, are quoted by kind permission of the University of Arizona Press, Tucson.

LIBRARY OF CONGRESS CATALOGING IN PUBLICATION DATA
Main entry under title:

Hogans.

   1. Navaho poetry — Translations into English.
2. Navaho Indians — Dwellings. 3. Indians of North
America — Southwest, New-Dwellings. I. McAllester,
David Park, 1916– II. McAllester, Susan W.,
1919–
PM2009.Z95E5 1980   897′.2   79-25075
ISBN 0-8195-6185-1

All inquiries and permissions requests should be addressed to the Publisher, Wesleyan University Press, 110 Mt. Vernon Street, Middletown, Connecticut 06457.

Distributed by Harper & Row Publishers, Keystone Industrial Park, Scranton, Pennsylvania 18512.

Manufactured in the United States of America

First printing, 1981
Wesleyan Paperback, 1987

Even today we have good examples to show that
without a hogan you cannot plan. You can't
just go out and plan other things for your future;
you have to build a hogan first. Within that,
you sit down and begin to plan.

— Frank Mitchell, in Navajo Blessingway Singer

CONTENTS

ACKNOWLEDGMENTS

Photographer's Thanks

For help with the pictures I thank, first of all, the people who welcomed me and allowed me to photograph the interiors of their homes, especially Augusta Sandoval of Chinle; Ethnobah Sandoval and A. G. Sandoval, Jr., of Lukachukai; Andy Jodi and Margaret B. Harvey, also of Lukachukai; and Lynn and Martha Huenemann of the Navajo Community College at Tsaile. The Wheelwright Museum in Santa Fe kindly allowed me to photograph copies of sand paintings in its collection. Carol Reck taught me to print photographs and Jean Cochrane provided me with the darkroom to do it in, and I am happy for this opportunity to thank them publicly.

David McAllester, my husband, introduced me to Navajos and their houses more than twenty years ago, had the idea for this book, and traveled with me to take the pictures. Each trip to the Southwest with him has made me eager for the next.

Translator's Thanks

After my formal training in music and anthropology I had the privilege of starting all over again, in the 1950's, with a new set of teachers. My gratitude goes most particularly to Frank Mitchell of Chinle; Albert G. Sandoval, Sr., and Albert G. Sandoval, Jr., of Lukachukai; Nat'áanii of Wupatki; and James Smith of Ganado. The Mitchell and Sandoval families, with their warm sympathy and hospitality, made those years of study a delight. I also owe a great debt to my non-Navajo colleagues in Navajo studies, especially Leland C. Wyman, Charlotte J. Frisbie, and, in treasured conversations and through their voluminous writings, Father Berard Haile, Clyde Kluckhohn, Gladys A. Reichard, and Mary C. Wheelwright. The narrative of the creation story that provides the framework for the presentation of the poems and photographs was drawn from Slim Curly's Blessingway myth, recorded by Fr. Berard Haile and edited by Leland C. Wyman.[1] I wish to thank Wyman and the University of Arizona Press for this, for the direct quotations from this work, and for access to Fr. Berard's recordings in Navajo from which three of my retranslations (see notes 27, 32, 35) were made. To Valborg Proudman go special thanks for the meticulous typing in English and Navajo that enabled us to see what the poems could really look like. She was a cheerful and willing companion in our labors.

Susan McAllester's good sense and critical eye have been invaluable since the beginning. Her presence in the field has added immeasurably to both the profit and the pleasure of ventures that would have been far more difficult without her. Her honest and powerful photographs are essential to a book on the houses of such an eminently visual people as the Navajos.

DAVID P. McALLESTER
SUSAN W. McALLESTER

HOGANS : Navajo Houses & House Songs

INTRODUCTION

Navajo Houses

The poetry in which the Navajos celebrate the hogan (literally "place home" or, simply translated, "house") is contained in songs and prayers numbering into the hundreds. Any Navajo home may become the locus of a ceremonial to bless its occupants and make them immune to sickness and danger. When this occurs, symbolic phrases are recited to dedicate the house for sacred use by identifying it with the homes of the most potent gods of the Navajo pantheon. The humble log structure will then become the first house ever to have been built on earth when the Holy People were planning the creation of the world as we know it today. It may be the home built for Changing Woman * when she was still a girl approaching maturity at Mountain-around-which-traveling-was-done (Huerfano Mesa in New Mexico). It may be the home of Changing Woman's celestial spouse, the Sun, who lives in the sky in a many-chambered dwelling where all kinds of game, livestock, singing birds, jewels, and beautiful fabrics can be seen. After Changing Woman and her warrior sons helped to cleanse the world of monsters, they moved to a replica of the Sun's house that he had prepared for them in the Western Ocean. There the Navajo clans of today were created and sent on their way to people the world. Blessingway, the central Navajo ceremony, was brought from Changing Woman's home in the West to benefit humankind.

There is nothing in any other published literature comparable to the songs and prayers that relate Navajo homes to these primordial and cosmic houses. House beams, reverently named Wood Woman, listen and fall into place at the command of gods. Houses made of dawn and afterglow with rooms of white shell and turquoise and fabrics of rainbow and yellow cloud spring from the imagination of these people who moved into the Southwest as nomads only a few hundred years ago.

In real life the hogan is the place where Navajo Indians make plans and in which they live as well as the place in which they hold their ceremonies. Until recent times a round one-room dwelling housed birth, sleeping, cooking, ceremonies, motherless lambs on the bottle—everything except death. Dying takes place, if possible, outside the house. Historically there have been two versions of the round one-room house. The first, called the "four-forked-beams hogan," was shaped like an inverted cone with a covered entryway. It was said to have been suggested by the hump at the end of Spruce Hill (Gobernador Knob in New Mexico), a steep little rise of ninety or a hundred feet where the baby Changing Woman was found. First Man and First Woman erected a house shaped like the mountaintop in which to take

---

* Changing Woman is the principal Navajo deity. Her name comes from the cycle of changes in her age: young in the spring, mature in the late summer, old in winter, and young again the following spring.

care of her. Later, when she moved into a house of her own, it was beside Mountain-around-which-traveling-was-done, a table-shaped formation which suggested the form of the hexagonal or octagonal cribbed-roof hogan that is still in use today. This building, in its basic form, has walls made of logs laid horizontally and chinked with clay. The top is closed in with cribbed logs up to the smoke hole, and the roof is covered with earth.

On the Navajo Reservation * now there are many types of buildings with specialized functions which are not dwellings: schools, stores, offices, hospitals, etc. Four dwelling-house plans are available from the tribal housing authority for those who wish assistance in putting up a house. One, a popular one, is a one-room dwelling of the same shape as the cribbed-roof hogan. But it has windows and electricity, and the sparkproof roof around the stovepipe is of roll roofing rather than of earth. Some establishments, particularly where there is a cluster of buildings belonging to different members of the same family, maintain a cribbed-roof hogan for ceremonies even though no one any longer lives in it regularly. Between times it may be used for storage or for penning lambs and young goats.

All of the pictures in this book, except those of the model log hogan beside the Headquarters of the Canyon de Chelly National Monument, are of buildings in use on the Navajo Reservation in the spring of 1977. Most of them are dwellings, often four- or five-room houses or mobile homes like off-reservation modern housing. Since the middle of the twentieth century the hogan shape has also been used for buildings which are not lived in: the meeting place of the Navajo Tribal Council; the Navajo Community College, where the campus ground plan is based on the interior floor plan of a hogan, and where most of the individual buildings are hogan-shaped as well; visitor centers at the main entries to the reservation; Christian churches; stores; etc. No photograph of the first shape, the four-forked-beam hogan with the covered entryway, is included here because it is no longer used. Some Navajos still live in the cribbed-roof hogan. It is a useful shape, well adapted to life in the high semidesert climate, and set close to the earth of which it is partly constructed. But Navajos who have shifted into the pattern of white culture are likely to form smaller family groupings, work at jobs away from home, and live in houses which are subdivided into rooms with specialized functions. Many have electricity or gas for cooking, but few have central heating. The stove, whether for cooking or for heating, remains actually and symbolically at the center of the house. Brush shelters, often erected initially to shade the cooking at ceremonies, continue to give breezy relief during the summer.

Both the chants and the houses are always changing. Some chants are no longer remembered, and some house forms are no longer used. But Navajos can now afford to pay for more performances of ceremonies than before, and there is a greater variety of house designs than before. The House

* Our largest Indian reservation: some 25,000 square miles spreading over western New Mexico, northern Arizona, and southern Utah.

Blessing itself is in frequent use because there are many new buildings to be blessed, but a shortened, streamlined version is now used.[2] The houses described in the long chants of the Navajos are fabulous; their actual living places are simple. In their traditional ceremonies they envision houses with cosmic ground plans, spacious structures of dawn, jewels, cloud—beautiful and appropriate substances, tangible or ephemeral. In a sense, this has freed the people to live simply; or, put another way, it has made hardship reasonable. This book juxtaposes the houses of the imagination in the songs with the houses of everyday life shown in the photographs. The contrast gives some hint of the range of the Navajo spirit.

Navajo House Songs

The poems that carry the magical house images were created in series of four or twelve or even as many as twenty or thirty songs, or in prayers in many sections that may take half an hour or longer to recite. The songs are usually performed in powerful *a capella* singing but may in some cases be accompanied by rattles of pebbles enclosed in rawhide or made of the tips of many deer hooves jingling together. Songs describing the Sun's house may be sung in the Shootingway or Red Antway ceremonials to the sound of drumming on a low basket turned over on the ground and struck with a heavy plaited yucca-leaf drumstick. The melody usually begins with a lyric chorus, moves on to a set of ten, twenty, or more verses chanted in a restricted tonal range, then a middle chorus, another set of verses balancing the first, and, finally, a concluding chorus. Usually every line in the verses ends with a burden derived from the latter part of the choruses. The first set of verses is often male in its symbolism and the second set female.

The prayers are intoned by the ceremonial practitioner in rapid cadences. The practitioner is echoed a syllable later, litany style, by the one-sung-over (translation of the Navajo term for the person for whom a ceremony is being performed). The voices and the rapt expressions of the participants leave no doubt that sacred words of great power are being used.

This book contains only a sampling of the house poems of the Navajos. They are translated from recordings made by Hastiin Tł'a'í, Frank Mitchell, Slim Curly, Hastiin Naat'áanii, and James Smith. I selected songs that would illustrate the role of houses in the creation story and that were also in complete enough form to do justice to the structure of traditional Navajo sung poetry. Long repetitions and nonlexical syllables (vocables or "nonsense" syllables) are usually omitted in printed translations because of publishing costs and the impatience of much of the reading public with repetitions and unfamiliar syllables that cannot be translated. Except for the transliterations of Hoijer, I had to go to sound recordings for the full texts. These elements of poetic expression have been preserved here. The aim has been to convey to the reader what the Navajos themselves are saying rather than to create translations which are comfortable to the ears of non-Navajos, and thus to extend to the reader the privilege of participating further than is usually possible in the beauty and vitality of the Navajo poetic world.

In my translations (and retranslations, pp. 22–24, 74, 80–82) I have also tried to retain Navajo word order as much as possible. To give the reader a sense of the choices facing the translator, I present here the first two lines of verse 1 of the First Construction Song (see p. 25) as it was sung by Naat'áanii. Vocables are indicated by italics. Under these lines I give the Navajo as it is spoken and in interlinear translation. Then follows a discussion of the free translations offered in this book.

Neye * Nahasdzaan*iye bila* bisadi   dooleł   *ye*   banatsidzikees   *'e-ye*,
Nohosdzáán   bisahdii dooleł   baa ntsídziikees
Earth Woman   her roof beam will be   of it   he is thinking

Tsi'isdzaan*iya*   sadi   dooleł *ye* banatsidzikees   *'e-ye* . . .
Tsin 'isdzáán   sahdii   dooleł   baa ntsídziikees
Wood Woman   roof beam   will be   of it   he is thinking

> *Neye*, Earth Woman, *'iye bila*, her roof beam to be, *ye*,
> About this, he is thinking, *'e-ye*,
> Wood Woman, *'iya*, the roof beam to be, *ye*,
> About this, he is thinking, *'e-ye* . . .

It is the ceremonial practitioner, of course, who knows the text best and can identify what is lexical and what is vocabalic. After Naat'áanii recorded the song he went over it line by line giving the lexical Navajo as it would be spoken. But the literal sentence in English still seems backward and ambiguous. A smooth and explicit free translation might read:

(The leader) is thinking about what Earth Woman's roof beam will be,
(The leader) is thinking about the roof beam to be, (named) Wood Woman.

* The pronunciation of the vocables is with continental vowel values. The reader will find variations, e.g.: *holaghei* and *halaghei*, *iye* and *eye*, etc. These follow the pronunciations of the singers in the recordings. Hyphens indicate a long note as the syllable was sung; "ŋ" is the soft ng as in "singing"; "gh" is a uvular sound like the French "r." The Navajo orthography used here is the LaFarge-Harrington alphabet: double vowels are long; speech tones are indicated by "accent" marks; "ł" is the unvoiced lateral "l" as in the Welsch "Flloyd"; "'" is a glottal stop as indicated by the hyphen in "oh-oh." For a fuller guide to Navajo pronunciation see Young and Morgan, pp. i–vi.[3]

This is understandable but hardly poetic. Moreover, in the Navajo word order the first impact is Earth Woman, not the leader, and "thinking" is a refrain that comes over and over again. As long as the meaning does not get lost, I have preferred to keep to the original progression of ideas, not just to give the translation a "Navajo flavor," but because word order is one of the linguistic clues to Navajo thinking.

In written English we have been trained to avoid uncertain referents. "He is thinking about it" does not tell us who is thinking about what. The Navajos, on the other hand, have been trained to a meticulous respect for privacy. Introductions and namings are felt by them to be intrusive, impolite, and even dangerous. I have kept the Navajo ambiguity in the translation and tried to satisfy the Anglo-European need to "know who" with a footnote based on Naat'áanii's answer when *I* needed to know.

My translation is partly in English and partly still in Navajo, since the vocables are preserved in their original form and position. I agree with the principle, most eloquently stated by Dell Hymes,[4] that vocables are by no means mere "nonsense syllables" but are an integral part of American Indian poetic style. Hymes pointed out that in Kwakiutl songs from the Northwest Coast vocabalic introductions prefigured in microcosm the structure of the poem as a whole. The same thing may be seen in Navajo song texts.[5] Other principles of patterning in Navajo vocables have been studied by Charlotte Frisbie.[6] Gladys Reichard has identified structural principles of Navajo traditional poetry as it appears in prayers,[7] and Sam Gill has made an analysis of the component parts in fifteen thousand lines of prayer texts.[8] A full-scale study of form in Navajo ritual poetry as sung remains to be undertaken.

Jerome Rothenberg has attempted a "total translation," including vocables, by following the sound-function of the vocables in the original Navajo. For example, the word "'eshkii" (boy) might have the vocables *i* and *ye* added ("'esh*i*ki*ye*") in song. The translation, "boyngnng" seeks to convey the distortion in the Navajo sung version and also link the word "boy" to the vocabalic refrain.[9] I have not felt sure enough of the intentions of the singers or my own poetic intuitions to follow this interesting idea.

THE FIRST HOUSE

At the Emergence Place, where the first beings came up from the underworld, First Man and First Woman created a young man and young woman from the inner forms of the heavenly bodies, from the four directions, from waters, mountains, plants—in fact, from the cosmos. The young couple were radiantly beautiful, with hair reaching to their thighs and voices like the singing of birds.

First Man said that the young man and woman were to be the source of all life and that they would never be seen on earth again. He then concealed them in his medicine bundle with coverings of dawn, twilight, sunlight, and darkness and set about creating the first house, the prototype of the homes where human lives would be centered in the future.

In Navajo philosophy, the material world is the result and also the manifestation of the power of sacred words. The words, in turn, proceed from thought, and behind thought lies knowledge.[10] The leaders in charge of the construction of the first house are the Sun, the Moon, Talking God, and Calling God. Their songs begin with a celebration of the knowledge, thinking, and speaking of the various places where the house materials are found. The sources of material are personified as Earth Woman and Mountain Woman, and the sustenance of future housedwellers as Water Woman and Corn Woman.

The young couple, it turns out, are named Long-life-returning and Causing-happiness-everywhere. They are the (briefly) visible forms of those two most potent phrases in all Navajo ceremonial poetry. It is they who give birth to Changing Woman, the principal Navajo deity and creator. Their names appear as a benediction and invocation of long life and happiness through all the literature of Blessingway songs.

'ai nai yaŋa,

> The places in times past, I knew all about them,
> The places in times past, I knew all about them,
> The places in times past, I knew all about them, *holaghai,*

Neye, Earth Woman, *yeye,*
> Where she would be, *deye,* I knew all about it, *'eye,*
All living plants, *'iye,*
> Where they would be, *deye,* I knew all about it, *'eye,*
All kinds of fabrics, *ye,*
> Where they would be, *deye,* I knew all about it, *'eye,*
Now, Long-life-returning, now, Causing-happiness-everywhere, *ne,*
> Where they would be, *deye,* I knew all about it, *'eye,*
>> The places in times past, I knew all about them, *holaghai;*

Neye, Mountain Woman, *'iye,*
> Where she would be, *deye,* I knew all about it, *'eye,*
The rainy mountains, *'iye,*
> Where they would be, *deye,* I knew all about it, *'eye,*
All kinds of jewels, *ye,*
> Where they would be, *deye,* I knew all about it, *'eye,*
Now, Long-life-returning, now, Causing-happiness-everywhere, *ne,*
> Where they would be, *deye,* I knew all about it, *'eye,*
>> The places in times past, I knew all about them, *holaghai;*

Neye, Water Woman, *'iye,*
> Where she would be, *daye,* I knew all about it, *'eye,*
The waters constantly flowing together, *'iye,*
> Where they would be, *deye,* I knew all about it, *'eye,*
Now, Long-life-returning, now, Causing-happiness-everywhere, *ne,*
> Where they would be, *deye,* I knew all about it, *'eye,*
>> The places in times past, I knew all about them, *holaghai;*

Neye, Corn Woman, *'iye*,
       Where she would be, *deye*, I knew all about it, *'eye*,
Corn pollen, *'iye*,
       Where it would be, *deye*, I knew all about it, *'eye*,
Now, Long-life-returning, now, Causing-happiness-everywhere, *ne*,
       Where they would be, *deye*, I knew all about it, *'eye*,
           The places in times past, I knew all about them;
           The places in times past, I knew all about them,
           The places in times past, I knew all about them,
           The places in times past, I knew all about them, *holagaŋane!*[11]

Leaders' House Songs: *Construction Song Number 1*

He ne yaŋa,

> About this, he is thinking,[12] *'e-ye*, about this, he is thinking, *'e-ye*,
> About this, he is thinking, *'e-ye*, about this, he is thinking, *'e-ye*,
> About this, he is thinking, *'e-ye*, about this, he is thinking, *'e-ye*,
> About this, he is thinking, *'e-ye*, about this, he is thinking, *holaghei;*

Neye, Earth Woman, *'iye bila*, her roof beam to be, *ye*,
> About this, he is thinking, *'e-ye*,
Wood Woman, *'iya*, the roof beam to be, *ye*,
> About this, he is thinking, *'e-ye*,
Now, Long-life-returning, now, Causing-happiness-everywhere, *ye*,
> The roof beam to be, *ye*,
> About this, he is thinking, *holaghei;*

Niyi, Mountain Woman, *'iye bila*, her roof beam to be, *ye*,
> About this, he is thinking, *'e-ye*,
Wood Woman, *'iya*, the roof beam to be, *ye*,
> About this, he is thinking, *'e-ye*,
Now, Long-life-returning, now, Causing-happiness-everywhere, *ye*,
> The roof beam to be, *ye*,
> About this, he is thinking, *holaghei;*

Neye, Water Woman, *'iye bila*, her roof beam to be, *ye*,
> About this, he is thinking, *'e-ye*,
Wood Woman, *'iya*, the roof beam to be, *ye*,
> About this, he is thinking, *e'ye*,
Now, Long-life-returning, now, Causing-happiness-everywhere, *ye*,
> The roof beam to be, *ye*,
> About this, he is thinking, *holaghei;*

Niyi, Corn Plant Woman, *'iye bila*, her roof beam to be, *ye*,
  About this, he is thinking, *'e-ye*,
Wood Woman, *'iya*, the roof beam to be, *ye*,
  About this, he is thinking, *'e-ye*,
Now, Long-life-returning, now, Causing-happiness-everywhere, *ye*,
  The roof beam to be, *ye*,
  About this, he is thinking, *'e-ye*,
 About this, he is thinking, *'e-ye*, about this, he is thinking, *'e-ye*,
 About this, he is thinking, *'e-ye*, about this, he is thinking, *hologhane!* [13]

'Eye neye yaŋa,

I plan it, *ni'eye ye*, I plan it, *ni'eya*,
I plan it, *ni'eye ye*, I plan it, *ni'eya*,
As I am planning, *wowo, wo*, just as I wish, *wo*,
Beautifully in place, it drops into position, *neyowo*,

The East, *'iye*, from under there to here, *ye*, my raised beam,
First, I lean it into position, *yi, she ye*,
Long-life-returning, *ye*, Causing-happiness-everywhere, *neye*,
As I am planning, *wowo, wo*, just as I wish, *wo*,
Beautifully in place, it drops into position, *neyowo*,

The West, *'iye*, from under there to here, *ye*, my raised beam,
Next, I lean it into position, *yi she ye*,
Long-life-returning, *ye*, Causing-happiness-everywhere, *neye*,
As I am planning, *wowo, wo*, just as I wish, *wo*,
Beautifully in place, it drops into position, *neyowo*,

The South, *'iye*, from under there to here, *ye*, my raised beam,
Between, I lean it into position, *yi she ye*,
Long-life-returning, *ye*, Causing-happiness-everywhere, *neye*,
As I am planning, *wowo, wo*, just as I wish, *wo*,
Beautifully in place, it drops into position, *neyowo*,

The North, *'iye*, from under there to here, *ye*, my raised beam,
The last one, I lean it into position, *yi she ye*,
Long-life-returning, *ye*, Causing-happiness-everywhere, *neye*,
As I am planning, *wowo, wo*, just as I wish, *wo*,
Beautifully in place, it drops into position, *neyowo*,

I plan it, *ni'eye ye*, I plan it, *ni'eya*,
I plan it, *ni'eye ye*, I plan it, *ni'eya*,
As I am planning, *wowo, wo*, just as I wish, *wo*,
Beautifully in place, it drops into position, *neyowo!* [14]

The chorus imitates laughter. Slim Curley said, "Those present were gladdened, they say; they laughed out loud."

> *He ne yaŋa,*
> Ye hiye heye-ye,
>> 'ai- yehiye, 'e- yehi ye-,
>> 'ai- yehiye, 'e- yehi yeye', *niyoŋoye,*
>
> Hiye, hiye yeye'
>> 'ai- yehiye, 'e- yehi ye-,
>> 'ai- yehiye, 'e- yehi yeye', *niyowo,*

The East, *'iye,* beneath it, from there to here, *ye*
> My raised beam, *ya,* I lean it first into position, *she-la,*
As I am planning for it, it drops into place,
As I am talking to it, it drops into place,
As it listens to me, it drops into place,
As Long-life-returning, it drops into place,
As Causing-happiness-everywhere, it drops into place,
> 'ai- yehiye, 'e- yehe yeye, *neyowo,*

The West, *'iye,* beneath it, from there to here, *ye,*
> My raised beam, *ya,* I lean it next into position, *she-la,*
As I am planning for it, it drops into place,
As I am talking to it, it drops into place,
As it listens to me, it drops into place,
As Long-life-returning, it drops into place,
As Causing-happiness-everywhere, it drops into place,
> 'ai- yehiye, 'e- yehe yeye, *neyowo,*

The South, *'iye*, beneath it, from there to here, *ye*,
> My raised beam, *ya*, I lean it into position between, *she-la*,
As I am planning for it, it drops into place,
As I am talking to it, it drops into place,
As it listens to me, it drops into place,
As Long-life-returning, it drops into place,
As Causing-happiness-everywhere, it drops into place,
> *'ai- yehiye, 'e- yehe yeye, neyowo*,

The North, *'iye*, beneath it, from there to here, *ye*,
> My raised beam, *ya*, I lean it into position last, *she-la*,
As I am planning for it, it drops into place,
As I am talking to it, it drops into place,
As it listens to me, it drops into place,
As Long-life-returning, it drops into place,
As Causing-happiness-everywhere, it drops into place,
> *'ai- yehiye, 'e- yehe yeye, neyowo*,

Placed below, *ŋi-la*,
As I am planning for it, it drops into place,
As I am talking to it, it drops into place,
As it listens to me, it drops into place,
As Long-life-returning, it drops into place,
As Causing-happiness-everywhere, it drops into place,
> *'ai- yehiye, 'e- yehe yeye, neyowo*,

Placed above, *ŋi-la*,
As I am planning for it, it drops into place,
As I am talking to it, it drops into place,
As it listens to me, it drops into place,
As Long-life-returning, it drops into place,
As Causing-happiness-everywhere, it drops into place,
> *'ai- yehiye, 'e- yehe yeye, neyowo*,
> *'ai- yehiye, 'e- yehiye-*,
> *'ai- yehiye, 'e-yehiyeye', neyowo!*[15]

'eye yeye yaŋa,

Here, *wowo-*, it is put in, *ye*, here, *wowo-*, it is put in, *ye*,
Here, *wowo-*, it is put in, *ye*, here, *wowo-*, it is put in, *ye*,

Here, *ŋa*, it is put in, *yaye*,
Here, *ŋa*, it is put in, *ŋa, halaghei,*

Neye, the East, *'iye*, the fire, *wowo*, it is put in, *ye*,
Wood Woman, the fire, *wo, wowo*, it is put in, *ye*,
Long-life-returning, the fire, *wo, wowo*, it is put in, *ye*,
Here, every kind of contentment, it is put in, *yeye*,
Here, *ŋa*, it is put in, *ŋa, halaghei,*

Neye, the South, *'iye*, the fire, *wowo*, it is put in, *ye*,
Wood Woman, the fire, *wo, wowo*, it is put in, *ye*,
Long-life-returning, the fire, *wo, wowo*, it is put in, *ye*,
Here, every kind of contentment, it is put in, *yeye*,
Here, *ŋa*, it is put in, *ŋa, halaghei,*

Neye, the West, *'iye*, the fire, *wowo*, it is put in, *ye*,
Wood Woman, the fire, *wo, wowo*, it is put in, *ye*,
Long-life-returning, the fire, *wo, wowo*, it is put in, *ye*,
Here, every kind of contentment, it is put in, *yeye*,
Here, *ŋa*, it is put in, *ŋa, halaghei,*

Neye, the North, *'iye*, the fire, *wowo*, it is put in, *ye*,
Wood Woman, the fire, *wo, wowo*, it is put in, *ye*,
Long-life-returning, the fire, *wo, wowo*, it is put in, *ye*,
Here, every kind of contentment, it is put in, *yeye*,
Here, *ŋa*, it is put in, *ŋa,*

Here, *wowo-*, it is put in, *ye*, here, *wo-*, it is put in, *ye*,

Here, *ŋa*, it is put in, *'aye,*
Here, *ŋa*, it is put in, *halaghane!* [16]

'Eye neye yaŋa,

I, *yeye 'eye,* I know about it, *ne,* I, *yeye yeye,* I know about it, *ye,*
I, *yeye yeye,* I know about it, *ne,* I, *yeye yeya,* I know about it, *ne,*
I, *yeye-ya,* I know about it, *ne, halaghei,*

Neye, my sacred home, *ye,* the doorpath before it, *ye,*
  They have come to be, it is asked, "Is it that?"
Now, Long-life-returning, now, *ye,* Causing-happiness-everywhere, *'iya,*
  They have come to be, it is asked, "Is it that?"

I, *yeye,* I know about it, *ni,* I, *yeye-ye,* I know about it, it is,
I, *yeye, yeye,* I know about it, *ni,*
I, *yeye ye,* I know about it, *ne, halaghei,*

Neye, my woven curtain, *niyeye,* now the stone set in place, *ye,*
  They have come to be, it is asked, "Is it that?"
Now, Long-life-returning, now, *ye,* Causing-happiness-everywhere, *'iya,*
  They have come to be, it is asked, "Is it that?"

I, *yeye,* I know about it, *ni,* I, *yeye-ye,* I know about it, it is,
I, *yeye, yeye,* I know about it, *ni,*
I, *yeye ye,* I know about it, *ne, halaghei,*

Neye, my fire, *ye,* my food, *'iye,*
  They have come to be, it is asked, "Is it that?"
Now, Long-life-returning, now, *ye,* Causing-happiness-everywhere, *'iya,*
  They have come to be, it is asked, "Is it that?"

I, *yeye,* I know about it, *ni,* I, *yeye-ye,* I know about it, it is,
I, *yeye, yeye,* I know about it, *ni,*
I, *yeye ye,* I know about it, *ne, halaghei,*

Neye, my pot, *'iyeye,* the stirring sticks, *'eye,*
  They have come to be, it is asked, "Is it that?"
Now, Long-life-returning, now *ye,* Causing-happiness-everywhere, *'iya,*
  They have come to be, it is asked, "Is it that?"

  I, *yeye,* I know about it, *ni,* I, *yeye-ye,* I know about it, it is,
  I, *yeye, yeye,* I know about it, *ni,*
  I, *yeye ye,* I know about it, *ne, halaghei,*

Neye, my earthen pot, *yeye,* my dipper, *'iye,*
  They have come to be, it is asked, "Is it that?"
Now, Long-life-returning, now, *ye,* Causing-happiness-everywhere, *'iye,*
  They have come to be, it is asked, "Is it that?"

  I, *yeye,* I know about it, *ni,* I, *yeye-ye,* I know about it, it is,
  I, *yeye, yeye,* I know about it, *ni,*
  I, *yeye ye,* I know about it, *ne, halaghei,*

Neye, my basket, *'eye,* the brush, *'eye,*
  They have come to be, it is asked, "Is it that?"
Now, Long-life-returning, now, *ye,* Causing-happiness-everywhere, *'iye,*
  They have come to be, it is asked, "Is it that?"

  I, *yeye,* I know about it, *ni,* I, *yeye-ye,* I know about it, it is,
  I, *yeye, yeye,* I know about it, *ni,*
  I, *yeye ye,* I know about it, *ne, halaghei,*

Neye, my metate, *'iyeye,* the mano, *ye,*
  They have come to be, it is asked, "Is it that?"
Now, Long-life-returning, now, *ye,* Causing-happiness-everywhere, *'iye,*
  They have come to be, it is asked, "Is it that?"

  I, *yeye,* I know about it, *ni,* I, *yeye-ye,* I know about it, it is,
  I, *yeye, yeye,* I know about it, *ni,*
  I, *yeye ye,* I know about it, *ne, halaghei,*

Neye, my resting place, *yeye*, my grass matting, *'iye*,
    They have come to be, it is asked, "Is it that?"
Now, Long-life-returning, now, *ye*, Causing-happiness-everywhere, *'iye*,
    They have come to be, it is asked, "Is it that?"

    I, *yeye*, I know about it, *ni*, I, *yeye-ye*, I know about it, it is,
    I, *yeye, yeye*, I know about it, *ni*,
    I, *yeye ye*, I know about it, *ne, halaghei*,

Neye, my fabrics of all kinds, *yeye*, my jewels of all kinds, *ye*,
    They have come to be, it is asked, "Is it that?"
Now, Long-life-returning, now, *ye*, Causing-happiness-everywhere, *'iye*
    They have come to be, it is asked, "Is it that?"

    I, *yeye*, I know about it, *ni*, I, *yeye-ye*, I know about it, it is,
    I, *yeye, yeye*, I know about it, *ni*,
    I, *yeye ye*, I know about it, *ne, halaghei*,

Now, Long-life-returning, now, Causing-happiness-everywhere, *'iye*,
    They are together, it is asked, "Is it that?"
    I, *yeye*, I know about it,

    I, *yeye*, I know about it, *ni*, I, *yeye-ye*, I know about it, it is,
    I, *yeye, yeye*, I know about it, *ni*, I, *yeye ye*, I know about it, *ni*,
    I, *yeye ye*, I know about it, *ne*, I, *yeye ye*, I know about it, *halaghane!* [17]

Leaders' House Songs: *Moving In Song Number 1*

He- ne- yaŋa,

   With this, they are moving in, *ŋa yaŋa,*
   With this, they are moving in, *ŋaŋa,*
   With this, they are moving in, *ŋaŋa ye,*
   With this, they are moving in, *ŋaŋa yaŋa,*

   With this, they are moving in, *yaŋa yeye,*
   With this, they are moving in, *naŋa,*
   With this, they are moving in, *naŋa ye,*
   With this, they are moving in, *yaŋa halaghei,*

Neye, Earth Woman, *i yeye,* with her help, they are moving in, *naŋa ye,*
   With this, they are moving in, *nani yeye,*
Wood Woman, *yeye, yaŋa,* with her, they are moving in, *naŋa yeye,*
All kinds of fabrics, *yeye,* with these, they are moving in, *yaŋa ye,*
   With these, they are moving in, *nani yeye,*
Now, Long-life-returning, now, Causing-happiness-everywhere,
   With these, they are moving in, *naŋa ye,*

   With these, they are moving in, *naŋa yaŋa,*
   With these, they are moving in, *yaŋa yeye,*
   With these, they are moving in, *naŋa,*
   With these, they are moving in, *naŋa ye,*
   With these, they are moving in, *yaŋa halaghei!*

Neye, Mountain Woman, *yeye,* with her help, they are moving in, *naŋa ye,*
   With this, they are moving in, *nani yeye,*
Wood Woman, *yeye, yaŋa,* with her, they are moving in, *naŋa yeye,*
All kinds of jewels, *yeye,* with these, they are moving in, *yaŋa ye,*
   With these, they are moving in, *nani yeye,*
Now, Long-life-returning, now, Causing-happiness-everywhere,
   With these, they are moving in, *naŋa ye,*

With these, they are moving in, *naŋa yaŋa,*
With these, they are moving in, *yaŋa yeye,*
With these, they are moving in, *naŋa,*
With these, they are moving in, *naŋa ye,*
With these, they are moving in, *yaŋa halaghei!*

Neye, Water Woman, *yeye,* with her help, they are moving in, *naŋa ye,*
With this, they are moving in, *nani yeye,*
Wood Woman, *yeye, yaŋa,* with her, they are moving in, *naŋa yeye,*
All kinds of waters constantly flowing together, *yaŋa ye,*
With these, they are moving in, *nani yeye,*
Now, Long-life-returning, now, Causing-happiness-everywhere,
With these, they are moving in, *naŋa ye,*

With these, they are moving in, *naŋa yaŋa,*
With these, they are moving in, *yaŋa yeye,*
With these, they are moving in, *naŋa,*
With these, they are moving in, *naŋa ye,*
With these, they are moving in, *yaŋa halaghei!*

Neye, Corn Plant Woman, *yeye,* with her help, they are moving in, *naŋa ye,*
With this, they are moving in, *nani yeye,*
Wood Woman, *yeye, yaŋa,* with her, they are moving in, *naŋa yeye,*
All kinds of pollen, *yeye,* with these, they are moving in, *yaŋa ye,*
With these, they are moving in, *nani yeye,*
Now, Long-life-returning, now, Causing-happiness-everywhere,
With these, they are moving in, *naŋa ye,*

With these, they are moving in, *naŋa yaŋa,*
With these, they are moving in, *yaŋa yeye,*
With these, they are moving in, *naŋa,*
With these, they are moving in, *naŋa ye,*
With these, they are moving in, *yaŋa holagha-ne!* [18]

Ne- ye- yaŋa,

> With you, we moved in, *wo*, with you, we moved in, *wa-*,
> With you, we moved in, *ŋaŋa-*, with you, we moved in, *ŋaŋa neyowo*,

> With you, we moved in, *wo*, with you, we moved in, *wa-*,
> With you, we moved in, *ŋaŋa-*, with you, we moved in, *ŋaŋa neyowo*,

Now, Earth Woman, with her help, we moved in with you, *ŋaŋa neyowo*,
> Wood Woman, with her, we moved in with you, *ŋaŋa neyowo*,
> All kinds of fabrics, *ye*, with these we moved in with you, *ŋaŋa neyowo*,
> Long-life-returning, *'e*, Causing-happiness-everywhere,
>> With these, we moved in with you, *ŋaŋa neyowo*,

>> With you, we moved in, *wo*, with you, we moved in, *wa-*,
>> With you, we moved in, *ŋaŋa-*, with you, we moved in, *ŋaŋa neyowo*.

Now, Mountain Woman, with her help, we moved in with you, *ŋaŋa neyowo*,
> Wood Woman, with her, we moved in with you, *ŋaŋa neyowo*,
> All kinds of jewels, *ye*, with these we moved in with you, *ŋaŋa neyowo*,
> Long-life-returning, *'e*, Causing-happiness-everywhere,
>> With these, we moved in with you, *ŋaŋa neyowo*.

>> With you, we moved in, *wo*, with you, we moved in, *wa-*,
>> With you, we moved in, *ŋaŋa-*, with you, we moved in, *ŋaŋa neyowo*.

Now, Water Woman, with her help, we moved in with you, *ŋaŋa neyowo*,
> Wood Woman, with her, we moved in with you, *ŋaŋa neyowo*,
> All kinds of waters constantly flowing together, *ye*, with these we
>> moved in with you, *ŋaŋa neyowo*,
> Long-life-returning, *'e*, Causing-happiness-everywhere,
>> With these, we moved in with you, *ŋaŋa neyowo*,

>> With you, we moved in, *wo*, with you, we moved in, *wa-*,
>> With you, we moved in, *ŋaŋa-*, with you, we moved in, *ŋaŋa neyowo*,

Now, Corn Plant Woman, with her help, we moved in with you, *ŋaŋa neyowo*,
    Wood Woman, with her, we moved in with you, *ŋaŋa neyowo*,
    All kinds of pollen, *ye*, with these we moved in with you, *ŋaŋa neyowo*,
    Long-life-returning, *'e*, Causing-happiness-everywhere,
        With these, we moved in with you, *ŋaŋa neyowo*,

        With you, we moved in, *wo*, with you, we moved in, *wa-*,
        With you, we moved in, *ŋaŋa-*, with you, we moved in, *ŋaŋaŋa neyowo!* [19]

Leaders' House Songs: *Talking God's Song Number 5*

Talking God bequeathed to humankind his own set of hogan songs, associated with Changing Woman's home at Mountain-around-which-traveling-was-done (see p. 14). Before this, however, at the first house, he expressed his pleasure at how beautifully it was made and his feeling that it would always be a sacred place. He ended his contribution to the Leaders' songs by identifying female deities as the source of the particular beauty and sacredness of the house.

'E- ne- yaŋa,

Ho-wo 'e-ye-ye-ho-, at a sacred place I have arrived, wo-
Yeya haŋa, at a sacred place I have arrived, howo 'e- yeye,
'eye ŋaŋa, at a sacred place I have arrived, ya howowo 'eyeye,
Naŋa howo, at a sacred place I have arrived, yaŋa halaghei.

Neye, Earth Woman, ye, at her house, indeed, I have arrived, yeye,
Wood Woman, ye, at her house I have arrived, yeye,
All kinds of fabrics, at their house I have arrived, yeye,
Now Long-life-returning, ye, now Causing-happiness-everywhere, ye,
At their house I have arrived, wo-,
Yeya haŋa, at a sacred place I have arrived, howowo 'e- yeye,
'eye haŋa, at a sacred place I have arrived, ye howowo 'eyeye,
Naŋa howo, at a sacred place I have arrived, yaŋa halaghei!

Neye, Mountain Woman, ye, at her house, indeed, I have arrived, yeye,
Wood Woman, ye, at her house I have arrived, yeye,
All kinds of jewels, at their house I have arrived, yeye,
Now Long-life-returning, ye, now Causing-happiness-everywhere, ye,
At their house I have arrived, wo-,
Yeya haŋa, at a sacred place I have arrived, howowo 'e- yeye,
'eye haŋa, at a sacred place I have arrived, ye howowo 'eyeye,
Naŋa howo, at a sacred place I have arrived, yaŋa halaghei!

Neye, Water Woman, *ye*, at her house, indeed, I have arrived, *yeye*,
Wood Woman, *ye*, at her house I have arrived, *yeye*,
All kinds of waters constantly flowing together, at their house
I have arrived, *yeye*,
Now Long-life-returning, *ye*, now Causing-happiness-everywhere, *ye*,
At their house I have arrived, *wo-*,
Yeya haŋa, at a sacred place I have arrived, *howowo 'e- yeye*,
'eye haŋa, at a sacred place I have arrived, *ye howowo 'eyeye*,
Naŋa howo, at a sacred place I have arrived, *yaŋa halaghei!*

Neye, Corn Plant Woman, *ye*, at her house, indeed, I have arrived, *yeye*,
Wood Woman, *ye*, at her house I have arrived, *yeye*,
All kinds of pollen, at their house I have arrived, *yeye*,
Now Long-life-returning, *ye*, now Causing-happiness-everywhere, *ye*,
At their house I have arrived, *wo-*,
Yeya haŋa, at a sacred place I have arrived, *howowo 'e- yeye*,
'eye haŋa, at a sacred place I have arrived, *ye howowo 'eyeye*,
Naŋa howo, at a sacred place I have arrived, *yaŋa halaghei!*[20]

He- ne- yaŋa,

> The woman, from her, *yawe- ye-yeye laŋa,* beauty radiates, *ya,*
> The woman, from her, *yawe- ne laŋa,* beauty, *halaghei;*

Neye, Earth Woman, *ye,* her house, *ye-ye-,*

> From its back corner, *yo we-ye, yela ŋana,* beauty radiates,
> Now, Long-life-returning, now, Causing-happiness-everywhere, *yela ŋana,*
>> Beauty radiates,
>
> The woman, from her, *yowe-ye, yela ŋana,* beauty radiates,
> The woman, from her, *yowe-ye, yela ŋaha,* beauty, *wo halaghei;*

Neye, Mountain Woman, *ye,* her house, *ye-ye-,*

> From the center, *yo we-ye, yela ŋana,* beauty radiates,
> Now, Long-life-returning, now, Causing-happiness-everywhere, *yela ŋana,*
>> Beauty radiates,
>
> The woman, from her, *yowe-ye, yela ŋana,* beauty radiates,
> The woman, from her, *yowe-ye, yela ŋaha,* beauty, *wo halaghei;*

Neye, Water Woman, *ye,* her house, *ye-ye-,*

> From the fireside, *yo we-ye, yela ŋana,* beauty radiates
> Now, Long-life-returning, now, Causing-happiness-everywhere, *yela ŋana,*
>> Beauty radiates,
>
> The woman, from her, *yowe-ye, yela ŋana,* beauty radiates,
> The woman, from her, *yowe-ye, yela ŋaha,* beauty, *wo halaghei;*

Neye, Corn Plant Woman, *ye,* her house, *ye-ye-,*

> From the door-corners, *yo we-ye, yela ŋana,* beauty radiates,
> Now, Long-life-returning, now, Causing-happiness-everywhere, *yela ŋana,*
>> Beauty radiates,
>
> The woman, from her, *yowe-ye, yela ŋana,* beauty radiates,
> The woman, from her, *yowe-ye, yela ŋaha,* beauty, *wo halaghei;*

Neye, Pollen, *ye*, its house, *ye-*,

    From the door-path, *yo we-ye, yela ŋana*, beauty radiates,
    Now, Long-life-returning, now, Causing-happiness-everywhere, *yela ŋana*,
        Beauty radiates,

    The woman, from her, *yowe-ye, yela ŋana*, beauty radiates,
    The woman, from her, *yowe-ye, yela ŋaha*, beauty, *wo halaghei;*

Neye, The Ripener, *ye*, its house, *ye-*,

    From all around it, *yo we-ye, yela ŋana*, beauty radiates,
    Now, Long-life-returning, now, Causing-happiness-everywhere, *yela ŋana*,
        Beauty radiates,

    The woman, from her, *yowe-ye, yela ŋana*, beauty radiates,
    The woman, from her, *yowe-ye, yela ŋaha*, beauty, *wo halaghai!*[21]

TALKING GOD'S HOUSE SONGS

Before people in the form we now know them lived on earth, those who came up from the underworld were established in villages under the guidance of First Man and First Woman, Talking God and Calling God, and the other deities. The people fell to quarreling, as they had in previous worlds, and one of these disputes led to the departure of the men to live separately from the women. During the separation the women gave birth to various monsters, which were ravaging the land by the time the people came together again.

To meet this emergency, Long-life-returning and Causing-happiness-everywhere, the inner forms of the earth, gave birth to a daughter. She was called Changing Woman, and her sons were the warrior twins who grew up to rid the world of the monsters. This baby girl was found by First Man and Talking God on the top of Spruce Hill, a small and especially sacred mountain which is considered to be the heart of the Navajo country.

> He [First Man] then set out for that point, he proceeded up its eastern slope to the summit. . . . At its very center he saw a massive dark cloud delivering a light drizzle of rain. Rainbows and sunrays hung suspended here and there . . . while cornbeetles were calling their *loo-ol* sounds. . . . The babe lay over there on a layer of crystal sand, smoothed out as nicely as possible by hand, as it were. Its eyes were perfectly black spots. There he met the one who was standing here at the rim of the summit. Excitedly Talking God held his hand over his mouth and continuously clapped his hands. . . . "Of course I would raise it on pollen, on pollen of evening twilight, darkness, sunlight, horizontal blue," he said. "What you say will never do, my granduncle. . . . That's only of use for applications on selves, whereas I, by feeding broth, will raise it with moist food," First Man said. So that was settled. Right nearby there stood a cliffrose bush. The bark of that he tore off and after placing a rainbow beneath it he laid the bark on that. He also had cloth of a suitable size in which he wrapped it, then laid the babe on the cliffrose bark. He then rolled it in a dark cloud and laced this with sunray.[22]

In four days she grew from infancy to puberty. At her first menses all the deities were assembled and the first puberty ceremony was performed. This was the second ceremony to be performed on this earth, and First Man and First Woman's house, where it took place, was consecrated with the Leaders' House Songs. This took place about fifty miles west of Spruce Hill at Mountain-around-which-traveling-was-done. This mesa is considered to be the lungs of the Navajo country and its shape is identified

with the perpendicular sides and round roof of the six- or eight-sided hogan of the late period of Navajo history.

At Changing Woman's second menses Talking God was put in charge of the second puberty ceremony and this time the hogan was consecrated with his songs. After that, Changing Woman's initiation to womanhood was complete and the form of the Navajo girls' ceremony was established for all time. Traditional Navajo families hold this same ceremonial celebration for a girl's first and second menses today. The usual practice is to consecrate the hogan with the Leaders' hogan songs for the first and Talking God's hogan songs for the second.

In the story Coyote, who had attended uninvited, objected to Talking God's plan to sing only four house songs:

> Now over there on the east side Talking God had set twelve white shell tail-feathers in a row, at the south side he set twelve turquoise tail-feathers, at the west side he had set twelve abalone shell tail-feather figures, at the north side he had set twelve jet tail-feather figures in a row.

Coyote pointed out that the inner forms of the four sacred mountains of the four cardinal directions also had the same number of tail feathers and said that these powerful deities already knew that there should likewise be twelve songs. So it was decided that there should be twelve songs in Talking God's set of house songs.

> "Don't you see these?" Coyote said. "To these you have made offerings. Do your tail-feathers even cause you to think? By means of these, things are made known to you, and Calling God has the same tail feathers," he said.[23]

60

Talking God's House Songs: *Number 1*

Heye neye yaŋa,

    Over here, the house, *eye laŋa*, it is a blessed house, *neye*,
    Over here, the house, *eye la*, it is a blessed house, *neye*,
    Over here, the house, *eye la*, it is a blessed house, *neye*,
    Over here, the house, *eye laŋa*, it is a blessed house, *holaghei;*

Neye, the East, *shiye*, under it, there, the house, *eye la*, it is a blessed house, *neye*,
    Now Talking God, his house, *eye la*, it is a blessed house, *neye*,
    Dawn, white, *ye*, made of it, his house, *eye la*, it is a blessed house, *neye*,
    Corn, white, *'iye*, made of it, his house, *eye la*, it is a blessed house, *neye*,
    Fabrics of all kinds, *ye*, made of them, his house, *eye la*, it is a blessed house, *neye*,
    Waters constantly flowing together, *ye*, made of them, his house, *eye la*,
        it is a blessed house, *neye*,
    Pollen, *ye*, made of it, his house, *eye la*, it is a blessed house, *neye*,
    Now Long-life-returning, now Causing-happiness-everywhere, his house, *eye la*,
        it is a blessed house, *neye*,

    Over here, the house, *eye la*, it is a blessed house, *neye*,
    Over here, the house, *eye laŋa*, it is a blessed house, *holaghei;*

Neye, the West, *shiye*, under it, there, the house, *eye la*, it is a blessed house, *neye*,
    Now Calling God, his house, *eye la*, it is a blessed house, *neye*,
    The afterglow, yellow, *ye*, made of it, his house, *eye la*, it is a blessed house, *neye*,
    Corn, yellow, *ye*, made of it, his house, *eye la*, it is a blessed house, *neye*,
    Jewels of all kinds, *ye*, made of them, his house, *eye la*, it is a blessed house, *neye*,
    Little waters, *ye*, made of them, his house, *eye la*,
        it is a blessed house, *neye*,
    Pollen, *ye*, made of it, his house, *eye la*, it is a blessed house, *neye*,
    Now Long-life-returning, now Causing-happiness-everywhere, his house, *eye la*,
        it is a blessed house, *neye*,

    Over here, the house, *eye la*, it is a blessed house, *neye*,
    Over here, the house, *eye la*, it is a blessed house, *holaghaŋane!*[24]

Heye neye yaŋa,

Over there, *wo,* the doorpath, *eye la,* a blessed path, *eye,*
Over there, *wo,* the doorpath, *eye la,* a blessed path, *eye,*
Over there, *wo,* the doorpath, *eye la,* a blessed path, *eye,*
Over there, *wo,* the doorpath, *eye la,* a blessed path, *holaghei;*

Neye, the East, *shiye,* under it there, *ye,* the doorpath, *eye la,*
     a blessed path, *eye,*
Now Talking God, his doorpath, *eye la,*
     a blessed path, *eye,*
Dawn, white, *iye,* the doorpath by it, *eye la,*
     a blessed path, *eye,*
Corn, white, *iye,* the doorpath by it, *eye la,*
     a blessed path, *eye,*
Fabrics of all kinds, *iye,* the doorpath by them, *eye la,*
     a blessed path, *eye,*
Waters constantly flowing together, *iye,* the doorpath by them, *eye la,*
     a blessed path, *eye,*
Pollen, *iye,* the doorpath by it, *eye la,*
     a blessed path, *eye,*
Now Long-life-returning, now Causing-happiness-everywhere, their doorpath, *eye la,*
     a blessed path, *eye,*

Over there, *wo,* the doorpath, *eye la,* a blessed path, *eye,*
Over there, *wo,* the doorpath, *eye la,* a blessed path, *holaghei;*

Neye, the West, *shiye,* under it there, *ye,* the doorpath, *eye la,*
     a blessed path, *eye,*
Now Calling God, his doorpath, *eye la,*
     a blessed path, *eye,*

Afterglow, yellow, *iye*, the doorpath by it, *eye la*,
    a blessed path, *eye*,
Corn, yellow, *iye*, the doorpath by it, *eye la*,
    a blessed path, *eye*,
Jewels of all kinds, *iye*, the doorpath by them, *eye la*,
    a blessed path, *eye*,
The little waters, *iye*, the doorpath by them, *eye la*,
    a blessed path, *eye*,
Pollen, *iye*, the doorpath by it, *eye la*,
    a blessed path, *eye*,
Now Long-life-returning, now Causing-happiness-everywhere, their doorpath, *eye la*,
    a blessed path, *eye*,

Over there, *wo*, the doorpath, *eye la*, a blessed path, *eye*,
Over there, *wo*, the doorpath, *eye la*, a blessed path, *holaghaŋane!*[25]

Talking God's House Songs: *Number 7*

Heye neye yaŋa,

On the path, I start off, *ŋaye,* on the path, I start off, *ŋayeye,*
On the path, I start off, *ŋaye,* on the path, I start off, *ŋayeye,*
On the path, I start off, *ŋa holaghei;*

Neye, the East, *shiye,* under it there, *ye,* on the doorpath,
I start off, *ŋaye,*
Now, Talking God, on the doorpath by it,
I start off, *ŋaye,*
The dawn, *'iye,* on the doorpath by it,
I start off, *ŋaye,*
White corn, *ye,* on the doorpath by it,
I start off, *ŋaye,*
Fabrics of all kinds, *'e-ye,* on the doorpath by them,
I start off, *ŋaye,*
Waters constantly flowing together, *'iye,* on the doorpath by them,
I start off, *ŋaye,*
Pollen, *'iye,* on the doorpath by it,
I start off, *ŋaye,*
Now Long-life-returning, now Causing-happiness-everywhere, on their doorpath,
I start off, *ŋaye,*

Before me, *yi,* at that place, *yi,* everywhere is blessed, *wone,*
Behind me, *yesh,* from there, *ye,* everywhere is blessed, *woleye,*

On the path, I start off, *ŋaye,* on the path, I start off, *ŋayeye,*
On the path, I start off, *ŋa holaghei;*

Neye, the West, *shiye*, under it there, *ye*, on the doorpath,

           I start off, *ŋaye*,

Now, Calling God, on the doorpath by it,

           I start off, *ŋaye*,

The afterglow, *'iye*, on the doorpath by it,

           I start off, *ŋaye*,

Yellow corn, *ye*, on the doorpath by it,

           I start off, *ŋaye*,

Jewels of all kinds, *'e-ye*, on the doorpath by them,

           I start off, *ŋaye*,

The little waters, *'iye*, on the doorpath by them,

           I start off, *ŋaye*,

Pollen, *'iye*, on the doorpath by it,

           I start off, *ŋaye*,

Now Long-life-returning, now Causing-happiness-everywhere, on their doorpath,

           I start off, *ŋaye*,

Behind me, *yesh*, from there, *ye*, everywhere is blessed, *woleye*,

Before me, *yi*, at that place, *yi*, everywhere is blessed, *wone*,

        On the path, I start off, *ŋaye*, on the path, I start off, *ŋayeye*,

        On the path, I start off, *ŋa holaghaŋa na-!* [26]

CHANGING WOMAN'S HOME AT
MOUNTAIN-AROUND-WHICH-TRAVELING-WAS-DONE

Now that Changing Woman was mature she was given her own house, a four-forked-beams hogan, at the foot of Moutain-around-which-traveling-was-done. Since the dangerous monsters were abroad, First Man surrounded the mountain with dark mirage on all four sides to protect her.

She traveled about a good deal, however, for the purpose of gathering firewood, and when she was on Spruce Hill, the place of her birth and discovery, she was miraculousy impregnated by sunray and water and gave birth to Enemy Slayer and Born-for-water. The twins grew rapidly, were instructed by various gods, and were hidden in crevices of Mountain-around-which-traveling-was-done when the dangerous monsters were around.

THE TWINS GO TO
THEIR FATHER'S HOUSE IN THE SKY

The twins were teased about who their father was and demanded to know from their mother. Changing Woman evaded their questions but finally told them he was the Sun. The twins set off to find their father in the sky and after many adventures and narrow escapes saw the Sun's house floating in a lake, flickering in the distance at though it were on fire.

As they were wondering how they could cross the water, Spider Man came to their help. He threw his web across and carpeted it with rainbow, over which they crossed.

They approached the house and its dangerous guards:

Songs of the Sun's House in the Sky

[1]   Here the place is dangerous,
                  Toward it I am going,

Now Changing Woman, her child, since that is who I am, toward it I am going,
The Sun, his home, to that place, toward it I am going,
Turquoise, made of it, his house, to that place,
Turquoise, made of it, the ladder, to that place, toward it I am going,
The Turquoise rattle, shaking, to that place, toward it I am going,
The Sun, where he lives, to that place, toward it I am going,
The Great Bear, dark, his doorguard, to that place, toward it I am going,
As he says, "Come close if you dare!" toward him,
When I speak he will be quiet,

Long-life-returning, Danger-all-around, now since these are who I am,

                  Toward it I am going, *hi ghi hi, paa!*

[2]   *Na*, along dangerous places,
                  Toward them I am on my way,

Now White Shell Woman, her child, since that is who I am, toward them I am on my way,
The Moon, his home, to that place, toward it I am on my way,
White shell, made of it, his house, to that place,
White shell, made of it, the ladder, to that place, toward it I am on my way,
The white shell rattle, shaking, to that place, toward it I am on my way,
The Moon, where he lives, to that place, toward it, I am on my way,
The Great Snake, dark, his doorguard, to that place, toward it I am on my way,
As he says, "Come close if you dare!" toward him,
When I speak he will be quiet,

Long-life-returning, Danger-all-around, now since these are who I am,

                  Toward it I am on my way, *hi ghi hi paa!* [27]

THE HOGAN AS A PLACE OF DANGER

A number of Navajo ceremonials can be performed either in a Holyway manner or in a Monsterway manner. The latter form is exorcistic: heavy stress is placed on protection from danger by invoking the aid of powerful supernatural allies. The power of the ceremony renders all who participate dangerous, as can be seen in this Monsterway Hogan song:

'eye ne yaŋa,
My home, *ŋaŋa yene,*
My home, *ŋaŋa neye ne,*
My home, *neye,*
Now, *ŋa,* it causes fear, *ye, halaghei!*

Neye, now Changing Woman, her son, since that is who I am, *niyi gowo,*
My home, *'aŋa,* it causes fear, *ye deye*

Now the Sun, *ye,* his son, since that is who I am, *niyi gowo,*
My home, *'aŋa,* it causes fear, *ye deye,*

Now the great bear, dark, *ye,* since that is who I am, *niyi gowo,*
My home, *'aŋa,* it causes fear, *ye, deye,*

Now the wind, dark, *ye,* since that is who I am, *niyi gowo,*
My home, *'aŋa,* it causes fear, *ye deye,*

Now flint, dark, *ye,* with this, *ye,* at my home, *ne,*
My home, *'a-,* it causes fear, *ye deye,*

My home, *ye,* now with its flash lightning, *wo,*
My home, *'a-,* it causes fear, *ye deye,*

My home, *ye,* with its dangerous powers, *wo,*
My home, *'a-,* it causes fear, *ye deye,*

Now zigzag lightnings, *ye,* four at a time flashing out from me, *ye,*
My home, *'a-,* it causes fear, *ye deye,*

It strikes, *dala*, it strikes away from me to where my enemy is, *'eya*
Those evil-minded ones, *ye*, with powers of witchcraft, go away from me crying, *yewo*,
      My home, *'a-*, it causes fear, *ye deye*,

It strikes, *dola*, all the way out from me, *ye*,
The evil-minded ones, *neye*, are bowing their heads, *yewo*,
      My home, *'a-*, it causes fear, *yi deye*,

Now the feather, living, *ye*, with me it is rising up, *yewo*,
      My home, *'a-*, it causes fear, *yi deye*,

Now Long-life-returning, now Danger-all-around, since that is who I am, *neye wo*,
      My home, *'aŋe ha*, it causes fear, *ye de*,

      My home, *ghana neye*,
      My home, *ghana neye na*,
      My home, *ŋa neye*,
      Now, *ne*, it causes fear, *'e- yeye he!* [28]

THE TWINS ARRIVE AT THE SUN'S HOUSE

'Ai nai yaŋa.

Heya 'eyei yelou daŋa, I have arrived, *ne 'eye,*
Heya 'eyei yelou daŋa, I have arrived, *ne 'eye,*
Heya 'eyei yelou daŋa, I have arrived, *ne 'eye,*
Heya 'eyei yelou daŋa, I have arrived, *ŋa holaŋai,*

Neye, now Changing Woman, her child, that's who I am, *yei yegowa,*
   daŋa, I have arrived, *ne 'eye,*
The east, *shiye,* underneath it there, *daŋa,* I have arrived, *ne 'eye,*
Now the Sun, at his house, *daŋa,* I have arrived, *ne 'eye,*
The dark water, *'iye,* where it is lying in position there,
   daŋa, I have arrived, *ne 'eye,*
Turquoise, the house made of it, floating there,
   daŋa, I have arrived, *ne 'eye,*
Turquoise, the ladder made of it, extending up there,
   daŋa, I have arrived, *ne 'eye,*
Turquoise, the rattle, shaking there,
   daŋa, I have arrived, *ne 'eye,*
A creature, spotted, *'iye,* lying before it there,
   daŋa, I have arrived, *ne 'eye,*
Turquoise, its footpath there, *daŋa,* I have arrived, *ne 'eye,*
Turquoise, made of it, the footprints there, *daŋa,* I have arrived, *ne 'eye,*
Turquoise, made of it, the sitting marks there, *daŋa,* I have arrived, *ne 'eye,*
Turquoise, made of it, the handprints there, *daŋa,* I have arrived, *ne 'eye,*

Now Long-life-returning, now Causing-happiness-everywhere,
   I, since that is who I am, *daŋa,* I have arrived, *ne 'eye,*

  Heya, 'eyei yelaŋa daŋa, I have arrived, *ŋa holaghai;*

Now Changing Woman, her grandchild, since that is who I am, *yei yegowa,*

      daŋa, I have arrived, *ne 'eye,*

The east, *shiye,* underneath it there, *daŋa,* I have arrived, *ne 'eye,*

Now the Moon, at his house, *daŋa,* I have arrived, *ne 'eye,*

The blue water, *'iye,* where it is lying in position there,

      daŋa, I have arrived, *ne 'eye,*

White shell, the house made of it, floating there,

      daŋa, I have arrived, *ne 'eye,*

White shell, the ladder made of it, extending up there,

      daŋa, I have arrived, *ne 'eye,*

White shell, the rattle, shaking there,

      daŋa, I have arrived, *ne 'eye,*

A creature, white, *'iye,* lying before it there,

      daŋa, I have arrived, *ne 'eye,*

White shell, its footpath there, *daŋa,* I have arrived, *ne 'eye*

White shell, made of it, the footprints there, *daŋa,* I have arrived, *ne 'eye,*

White shell, made of it, the sitting marks there, *daŋa,* I have arrived, *ne 'eye,*

White shell, made of it, the handprints there, *daŋa,* I have arrived, *ne 'eye,*

Now Long-life-returning, now Causing-happiness-everywhere,

      I, since that is who I am, *daŋa,* I have arrived, *ne 'eye,*

    Heya 'eyei yelou daŋa, I have arrived, *ne 'eye,*
    Heya 'eyei yelou daŋa, I have arrived, *ne 'eye,*
    Heya 'eyei yelou daŋa, I have arrived, *ne 'eye,*
    Heya 'eyei yelou daŋa, I have arrived, *ne 'eye,*
    Heya 'eyei yelou daŋa, I have arrived, *ŋa golaghaŋane!* [29]

SONG OF THE SUN'S HOUSE

In the Shootingway ceremonial a model of the Sun's house is actually constructed. A painted screen of perpendicular wooden rods lashed side by side is tied to a stout pole framework and decorated with images of the Sun and three other deities of the sky: Moon, Dark Wind, and Yellow Wind. Clouds hover over the house and birds sing in the air above it. There are four doors through which guardian snakes issue and then slowly draw back again. The birds are made to sing and move in the air and the snakes are made to move in the doorway by assistants behind the Sun's house screen. As this complex symbolic representation is being constructed, the following song is sung. It describes the Sun's house and enumerates the sacred points leading to it and within it. Everyone present is given power by being symbolically dressed in the jewel substances from which the house is made.

'Eya neye yeye yaŋa,

Happiness, *yeye naŋa,* happiness, *yeye nam,*
It carries me, it carries me, *deye neye yaŋa,*
Happiness, *yeye naŋa,* happiness, *yeye nam,*
It carries me, it carries me, *deye neye yaŋa,*

The east, under it, *'ana,* from there
Now the Sun, *ye,* his house, *'aŋa, deye*
Turquoise, made of it, his house, floating, *yeye,*
Turquoise, made of it, the flooring, *'aŋa da,*
Turquoise, made of it, the ladder extending up, *'aŋa deye*
Dawn, *'iye,* now its pollen, *'iye,* of this kind is the doorpath, *yiyi deye*
Turquoise, your moccasins being that,
Turquoise, your leggings being that,
Turquoise, your clothing being that,
Turquoise feathers, *'iye,* your feathers being that,
Now birds, blue, your mind, *'eye,* carrying it for you,

Your house, toward it, the roads, *yish deye,*
Your house, toward it, the lookout point, *yish deye,*
Your house, toward it, the doorpath, *yish deye,*
Your house, its door corners, *hash deye,*

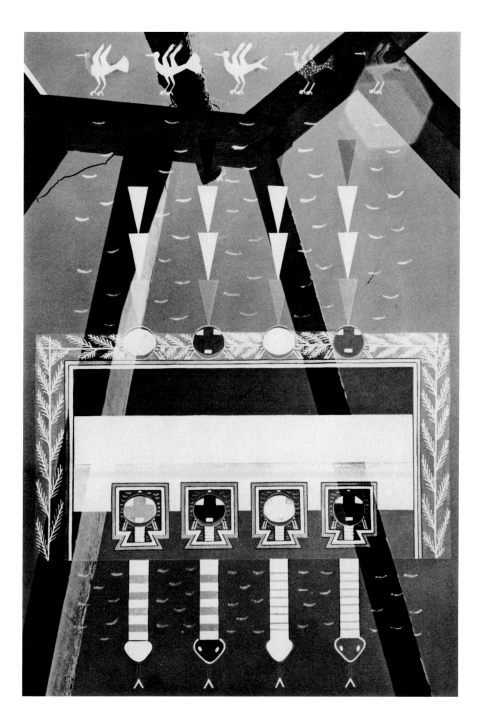

Your house, the fireside, *hash deye,*
Your house, the very center, *yish deye,*
Your house, the very back corner, *naŋa deye,*

Those things, *yeye- naŋa,* beautiful, *neye naŋa,*
        They carry me, they carry me, *dayei, neye yaŋa,*

The west, under it, *'ana,* from there,
Now the Moon, *ye,* her house, *yeye,*
White shell, made of it, her house, floating, *yeye,*
White shell, made of it, the flooring, *'aŋa da,*
White shell, made of it, the ladder extending up, *'aŋa deye,*
Yellow twilight, *'iye,* now its pollen, *'iye,* of this kind is the doorpath, *yiyi deye,*
White shell, your moccasins being that,
White shell, your leggings being that,
White shell, your clothing being that,
White shell feathers, *'iye,* your feathers being that,
Now birds, yellow, your mind, *'eye,* carrying it for you,

Your house, toward it, the roads, *yish deye,*
Your house, toward it, the lookout point, *yish deye,*
Your house, toward it, the doorpath, *yish deye,*
Your house, its door corners, *hash deye,*
Your house, the fireside, *hash deye,*
Your house, the very center, *yish deye,*
Your house, the very back corner, *naŋa deye,*

Those things, *yeye- naŋa,* beautiful, *neye naŋa,*
        They carry me, they carry me, *dayei, neye yaŋa,*

The south, under it, *'aŋa,* from there,
Now the Dark Wind, *ye,* his house, *'aŋa, deye,*
Abalone shell, made of it, his house, floating, *yeye,*
Abalone shell, made of it, the flooring, *'aŋa da,*
Abalone shell, made of it, the ladder extending up, *'aŋa deye,*
Dawn, *'iye,* now its pollen, *'iye,* of this kind is the doorpath, *yiyi deye,*
Abalone shell, your moccasins being that,

Abalone shell, your leggings being that,
Abalone shell, your clothing being that,
Abalone shell feathers *'iye*, your feathers being that,
Now tanagers, your mind, *'eye*, carrying it for you,

Your house, toward it, the roads, *yish deye*,
Your house, toward it, the lookout point, *yish deye*,
Your house, toward it, the doorpath, *yish deye*,
Your house, its doorcorners, *hash deye*,
Your house, the fireside, *hash deye*,
Your house, the very center, *yish deye*,
Your house, the very back corner, *naŋa deye*,

Those things, *yeye- naŋa*, beautiful, *neye naŋa*,
        They carry me, they carry me, *dayei, neye yaŋa*,

The north, under it, *'aŋa*, from there,
Now the Yellow Wind, *ye*, her house, *'aŋa deye*,
Coral, made of it, her house, floating, *yeye*,
Coral, made of it, the flooring, *'aŋa da*,
Coral, made of it, the ladder extending up, *'aŋa deye*,
Yellow Twilight, *'iye*, now its pollen, *'iye*, of this kind is the doorpath, *yiyi deye*,
Coral, your moccasins being that,
Coral, your leggings being that,
Coral, your clothing being that,
Coral feathers, *'iye*, your feathers being that,
The Ripener,* your mind, *'eye*, carrying it for you,

Your house, toward it, the roads, *yish deye*,
Your house, toward it, the lookout point, *yish deye*,
Your house, toward it, the doorpath, *yish deye*,
Your house, its doorcorners, *hash deye*,
Your house, the fireside, *hash deye*,
Your house, the very center, *yish deye*,
Your house, the very back corner, *naŋa deye*,

* A god associated with the ripening of corn, and often paired with Pollen Boy. It has been referred to as "grasshopper," "corn bug," and, most often, "corn-beetle" in the literature (see p. 110). I have preferred a translation closer to the Navajo, " 'Ańłt'ánii," "the Ripener."

Those things, *yeye- naŋa*, beautiful, *neye naŋa*,
      They carry me, they carry me, *dayei, neye naŋa*,

Happiness, *yeye naŋa*, happiness, *yeye nam*,
It carries me, it carries me, *deye neye yaŋa*,
Happiness, *yeye naŋa*, happiness, *yeye nam*,
It carries me, it carries me, *deya neye yaŋa holaghei*.[30]

THE TWINS ARE ACCEPTED BY THEIR FATHER

When the twins had proved to the Sun that they were indeed his children, they were dressed in turquoise and white shell and made beautiful like the sons and daughters who were already there in the house in the sky. There were stools of white shell, turquoise, abalone shell, and jet, and the twins sat down while the Sun offered them whatever they might want to take home with them.

When he offered them the wealth of jewels and the perfect shell discs hanging on the walls, the twins said, "We two did not come here for those things, our father."

They were then shown four great rooms, in the four directions, in which there were rain, rainbows, flowers, the singing of small birds, all kinds of wild game, horses, and sheep. As they looked through the white shell door, the turquoise door, the abalone shell door, and the jet door, they said each time, "We two did not come here for those things, our father."

Finally they revealed that they came for the flint armor and the weapons of lightning needed to rid the world of monsters. These the Sun parted with reluctantly, since some of the monsters were his own children. The twins then returned to earth with the help of the Sun, by means of rainbows, sunrays, and shafts of morning and evening twilight.

CHANGING WOMAN'S HOUSE IN THE WEST

When the world had been cleansed of monsters, Changing Woman's initial tasks of creation were completed and she called the last great assembly of the gods, at Mountain-around-which-traveling-was-done. It was announced that she was leaving this world to be established in a home on the western ocean that the Sun had made ready for her.

So that she would not be alone, twelve Turquoise Boys were created to accompany her. They were consecrated in a night-long Blessingway ceremony, and the time approached for her departure.

> As dawn approached from yonder, the dark cloud and the dark fog by means of which our mother was to go west were spread out. "Now I will go, my children, I will go in a sacred way, but I will always be among all of you," she said to them.
>
> Then the twelve Turquoise Boys who had been made went with her onto the dark cloud, it is said. Then the dark cloud rose with them, the dark fog also lifted with them. It went above the mountains. Those who were Talking God People set out after them. When the dark cloud rose, it circled with them four times in a sunwise direction. Then it set out with them toward the west. The small birds began singing more than ever before.[31]

Changing Woman's Arrival at Her House in the West

'Ene- ya- ye,

     Now I have arrived, *oye,*
     Now I have arrived, *ya- e-,*

White Shell Woman, since that is who I am, now I have arrived, *ya- e-,*
     Truly, below the west, at that place, now I have arrived, *ya- e-,*
     Truly, the end of the earth, at that place, now I have arrived, *ya- e-,*
     Truly, the end of the sky, at that place, now I have arrived, *ya- e-,*
     Truly, as far as the moon goes, at that place, now I have arrived, *ya- e-,*

Truly, where its dark water lies spread out, at that place, now I have arrived, *ya- e-,*
The white shell house floating, at that place, now I have arrived, *ya- e-,*
The white shell rooms, at that place, now I have arrived, *ya- e-,*
The white shell ladder, at that place, now I have arrived, *ya- e-,*
The white shell rattle, now moving itself, at that place, now I have arrived, *ya- e-,*
The white shell pathway, at that place, now I have arrived, *ya- e-,*
The white shell floor, on top of it, at that place, now I have arrived, *ya- e-,*
The white shell footprints, on top of them, at that place, now I have arrived, *ya- e-,*
     White shell being my moccasins, now by means of them I have arrived, *ya- e-,*
     White shell being my leggings, now by means of them I have arrived, *ya- e-,*
     White shell being my garments, now by means of them I have arrived, *ya- e-,*
     White shell being my headdress, now by means of it I have arrived, *ya- e-,*

White shell increasing, at the house of it, now I have arrived, *ya- e-,*
     White shell being my corn, by means of it, now I have arrived, *ya- e-,*
     White shell being my livestock, by means of them, now I have arrived, *ya- e-,*
     White shell being my baskets, by means of them, now I have arrived, *ya- e-,*

Truly, by these means, I myself having been changed into white shell,
     by means of it, now I have arrived, *ya- e-,*
Long-life-returning, Causing-happiness-everywhere, since these are what I am,
     now I have arrived, *ya- e-,*

Before me, at that place, everywhere being blessed, now I have arrived, *ya- e-*,
Behind me, at that place, everywhere being blessed, now I have arrived, *ya- e-*,

Now I have arrived, *oye*,
Now I have arrived, *ya- e-*, *ni- yo- o.*

Boy-with-whom-Dawn-appears, since that is who I am, now I have arrived, *ya- e-*,
Truly, below the east, at that place, now I have arrived, *ya- e-*,
Truly, the end of the sky, at that place, now I have arrived, *ya- e-*,
Truly, the end of the earth, at that place, now I have arrived, *ya- e-*,
Truly, as far as the sun goes, at that place, now I have arrived, *ya- e-*,

Truly, where its blue water lies spread out, at that place, now I have arrived, *ya- e-*,
The turquoise house floating, at that place, now I have arrived, *ya- e-*,
The turquoise rooms, at that place, now I have arrived, *ya- e-*,
The turquoise ladder, at that place, now I have arrived, *ya- e-*,
The turquoise rattle, now moving itself, at that place, now I have arrived, ya- e-,
The turquoise pathway, at that place, now I have arrived, *ya- e-*,
The turquoise floor, on top of it, at that place, now I have arrived, *ya- e-*,
The turquoise footprints, on top of them, at that place, now I have arrived, *ya- e-*,
Turquoise being my moccasins, now by means of them I have arrived, *ya- e-*,
Turquoise being my leggings, now by means of them I have arrived, *ya- e-*,
Turquoise being my garments, now by means of them I have arrived, *ya- e-*,
Turquoise being my headdress, now by means of them I have arrived, *ya- e-*,

Turquoise increasing, at the house of it, now I have arrived, *ya- e-*,
Turquoise being my corn, by means of it, now I have arrived, *ya- e-*,
Turquoise being my livestock, by means of them, now I have arrived, *ya- e-*,
Turquoise being my baskets, by means of them, now I have arrived, *ya- e-*,

Truly, by these means, I myself having been changed into turquoise,
by means of it, now I have arrived, *ya- e-*,
Long-life-returning, Causing-happiness-everywhere, since these are what I am,
now I have arrived, *ya- e-*,
Behind me, at that place, everywhere being blessed, now I have arrived, *ya- e-*,
Before me, at that place, everywhere being blessed, now I have arrived, *ya- e-*,

Now I have arrived, *oye*,
Now I have arrived, *ya- e-*, *ni- yo- o.*[32]

98

HOW BLESSINGWAY WAS GIVEN TO THE EARTH PEOPLE

And Changing Woman left for the west. A house had been built for her, designed in various colors on the outside, and inside a ladder had been provided. At this ladder a rattle had been set which would shake to let it be known that people had entered. White shell had been spread out and the floor space was white shell. In various places her footprints of white shell had been placed. And along the shore [of the Pacific Ocean] white shell had been washed [up] on the banks with turquoise, abalone, and jet. The purpose of this was that she would live by the strength of this food. And too a white shell cornstalk and a turquoise cornstalk were set at her entrance and were made as uprights of the entrance. Their purpose was to make things known to her. Pollen flowed down on the one to the east and on the one to the west. So at the tip of the one a bluebird regularly gave its call, at the tip of the other a corn-beetle regularly called. One would call regularly in the morning, the other at noon, one in the evening, another at midnight, and one at dawn. They had been made to do just that.

She had been made so that a change would come upon her every six months, she would then become young again. In this shape she reached the place which had been prepared for her. Now whenever the Sun was nearby returning to her that rattle would sound [before] he would enter. She had brought only the white shell and the turquoise basket with her to this place. At the very rear of the room the footprint figures and sitting place figures of Monster Slayer and Born for Water had been made, one of white shell, the other of turquoise. And on the south side there was another opening [to a room] in which a home had been prepared for the two to live. After their mother had arrived over there the two immediately followed her there. They had lived at Parallel Streams only for a short period. When they overtook their mother they merely motioned over those sitting place and footprint figures, then entered the home that had been prepared for them.

Meanwhile she had placed the baskets side by side between the seat figures of Monster Slayer and Born for Water. The turquoise basket she set toward Monster Slayer's side, the white shell one on the other side. Here she placed in them that medicine bundle which First Man formerly would never lay aside. Monster Slayer would stand on those footprint figures of his and would speak twice or three times about future conditions on the surface of this earth. He might do this four times, but that was a limit he would not exceed. That was the purpose of those footprint figures. And on the east side the Sun had placed up on a shelf the figure of a standing horse, and one on the south, west, and north sides. That, to an extent, explains why elders greatly value horse images. So you see the place was in this shape.[33]

Word reached the deities at Changing Woman's home in the west that things were going badly on earth. People were quarreling and killing each other and forgetting the instructions they had been

given by the deities. It was determined to carry off two young boys so that Changing Woman could instruct them in Blessingway. With this ceremony, the Earth People could live in harmony. When the boys had been suitably prepared, they came to the ocean shore overlooking Changing Woman's house:

> As they went along rainbows spread along in front of them and any number of rainbows were curved, one above the other. Now along the water surface they found that the house had floated close by and now stood here by the shore. Moreover, the designed outer surface of this house shone out in brilliant light. Nonetheless, the rainbow extended into the interior and on this they made their entry. Here, on a white shell ladder, was the entrance trail. Inside, there was a white shell trail leading in.[34]

Changing Woman showed them her eternal progression through maturity to old age and back again to young womanhood and then opened the doors to four great chambers around the central room where rain, flowers, wild game, and all domestic animals were teeming. She instructed the boys in the future use of all these things for mankind and then began to teach them the Blessingway. She told them the use of the Leaders' House Songs from the first ceremony at the edge of the Emergence Place, and Talking God's House Songs, and all the other parts of Blessingway. After the ceremonial bath, when she was drying herself with cornmeal, she created the first clans of the Navajo people from the mixture of the drying powder and her own outer skin. Then she showed the newly created people and the Crystal Boys the bounty with which they were to return to the earth.

Song of Changing Woman's Gifts to the People

'Ai 'ai na,

For a beautiful thing I came and waited,
For a beautiful thing I came and waited, *ni yo 'o,*

Now Changing Woman, her child, since that is who I am, I came and waited,
Now Changing Woman, her home, at the center of it, there I came and waited,
The white shell room, at the center of it, there I came and waited,
The white shell floor, precisely upon it, there I came and waited,
The white shell footprints, precisely upon them, there I came and waited,

Now Changing Woman, her pet, the white shell horse, for this I came and waited,
The coyote robe, its child, my child, for this I came and waited,
The white robe, its child, my child, for this I came and waited,
Now the white cotton sash, its child, my child, for this I came and waited,
Now the white buckskin, its child, my child, for this I came and waited,
Now the radiant doeskin, its child, my child, for this I came and waited,
Now the dark sewn fabric, its child, my child, for this I came and waited,
The white patched sash, its child, my child, for this I came and waited,
The many-colored sash, its child, my child, for this I came and waited,
Now the narrow white beads, their child, my child, for this I came and waited,
Now the many-formed beads, their child, my child, for this I came and waited,
White shell, its child, my child, for this I came and waited,
Turquoise, its child, my child, for this I came and waited,
Ear pendants, their child, my child, for this I came and waited,

The dark bow, its child, my child, for this I came and waited,
Now the tail-feathered arrow, its child, my child, for this I came and waited,
The mountain lion, its child, my child, for this I came and waited,
The perfect shell disk, its child, my child, for this I came and waited,
The great bead, its child, my child, for this I came and waited,
The red abalone shell, its child, my child, for this I came and waited,

104

Fabrics, all kinds of them, their child, my child, for this I came and waited,
Jewels, all kinds of them, their child, my child, for this I came and waited,
Horses, all kinds of them, their child, my child, for this I came and waited,
Sheep, all kinds of them, their child, my child, for this I came and waited,

This day they have made me their partner, thereby I am truly the gainer, my child,
     for this I came and waited,
Always increasing, never diminishing, my child, for this I came and waited,
Now Long-life-returning, now Causing-happiness-everywhere, since these are what I am, my child,
     for this I came and waited,
Behind me, everywhere being blessed, my child, for this I came and waited,
Before me, everywhere being blessed, my child, for this I came and waited,

     For a beautiful thing I came and waited,
     For a beautiful thing I came and waited, *ni yo 'o,*

Now the Sun, his child, since that is who I am, I came and waited,
Now the Sun, his home, at the center of it, there I came and waited,
The turquoise room, at the center of it, there I came and waited,
The turquoise floor, precisely upon it, there I came and waited,
The turquoise footprints, precisely upon them, there I came and waited,

Now the Sun, his pet, the turquoise horse, for this I came and waited,
The coyote robe, its child, my child, for this I came and waited,
The white robe, its child, my child, for this I came and waited,
The white cotton sash, its child, my child, for this I came and waited,
The white buckskin, its child, my child, for this I came and waited,
The radiant doeskin, its child, my child, for this I came and waited,
The dark sewn fabric, its child, my child, for this I came and waited,
The white patched sash, its child, my child, for this I came and waited,
The many-colored sash, its child, my child, for this I came and waited,
Now the narrow white beads, their child, my child, for this I came and waited,
Now the many-formed beads, their child, my child, for this I came and waited,
Turquoise, its child, my child, for this I came and waited,
White shell, its child, my child, for this I came and waited,
Ear pendants, their child, my child, for this I came and waited,

The mahogany bow, its child, my child, for this I came and waited,
Now the yellow-feathered arrow, its child, my child, for this I came and waited,
Now the otter, its child, my child, for this I came and waited,
The perfect shell disk, its child, my child, for this I came and waited,
The great bead, its child, my child, for this I came and waited,
The red abalone shell, its child, my child, for this I came and waited,

Jewels, all kinds of them, their child, my child, for this I came and waited,
Fabrics, all kinds of them, their child, my child, for this I came and waited,
Horses, all kinds of them, their child, my child, for this I came and waited,
Sheep, all kinds of them, their child, my child, for this I came and waited,

This day they have made me their partner, thereby I am truly the gainer, my child,
        for this I came and waited,
Always increasing, never diminishing, my child, for this I came and waited,
Now Long-life-returning, now Causing-happiness-everywhere, since these are what I am, my child,
        for this I came and waited,
Behind me, everywhere being blessed, my child, for this I came and waited,
Before me, everywhere being blessed, my child, for this I came and waited,

        For a beautiful thing I came and waited,
        For a beautiful thing I came and waited, *ni yo 'o*.[35]

NOTES

1. Wyman, Leland C., *Blessingway*. University of Arizona Press, Tucson, 1970.
2. Frisbie, Charlotte J., "The Navajo House Blessing Ceremonial." (Ph.D dissertation, University of New Mexico, Department of Anthropology). University Microfilms, Ann Arbor, 1970.
3. Young, Robert W. and William Morgan, *The Navaho Language*. Deseret Book Company, Salt Lake City, 1958.
4. Hymes, Dell, "Some North Pacific Coast Poems: A Problem in Anthropological Philology," *American Anthropologist*, vol. 67, no. 2, 1965, pp. 316–341.
5. McAllester, David P., "The First Snake Song," in *Festschrift for Gene Weltfish*, in press, cited in Gary Witherspoon, *Language and Art in the Navajo Universe*, University of Michigan Press, Ann Arbor, 1977, pp. 155–156.
6. Frisbie, Charlotte J., *Kinaaldá, A Study of the Navaho Girl's Puberty Ceremony*, Wesleyan University Press, Middletown, Connecticut, 1967, pp. 177–179.
7. Reichard, Gladys A., *Prayer: The Compulsive Word*, J. J. Augustin, Inc., New York, 1944.
8. Gill, Sam, "A Theory of Navajo Prayer Acts: A Study of Ritual Symbolism." (Ph.D. dissertation, University of Chicago, Divinity School). University Microfilms, Ann Arbor, 1974, p. 34.
9. Rothenberg, Jerome, "An Experiment in the Presentation of American Indian Poetry," in *Stony Brook* 3/4, 1969, pp. 292–305.
10. Witherspoon, pp. 29–46, 47–62.
11. Hastiin Tł'a'í (Klah), *Creation Chant Texts*, pp. 66–69, cylinder 40, song lla, recorded by Mary C. Wheelwright about 1925, transcribed and translated by Harry Hoijer. The cylinders are now in the Library of Congress; copies of the texts are deposited at the Wheelwright Museum, Santa Fe, New Mexico, and in the Archives of World Music, Wesleyan University, Middletown, Connecticut.

    Slim Curly (Wyman, p. 113) begins his Leaders' House Songs with this and three others. Hastiin Tł'a'í's recordings have almost identical texts but he listed them simply as "Hogan Songs," and did not include them in the set he entitled "Leaders' Hogan Songs." I have used the Tł'a'í version here since all the vocables are available in the transcription. My retranslation is according to the principles stated on pp. 16–17.
12. "He" here refers to one of the leaders; see p. 16.
13. Nat'áanii, *Blessingway Texts*, p. 24, reel 19, song 1, recorded by David P. McAllester, 1950. The tapes are desposited in the Archives of World Music, Wesleyan University. This was his first Leaders' House Song; it is also the first for Frank Mitchell (Frisbie, 1967, pp. 111–117).
14. Naat'áanii, p. 24, reel 20, song 1.
15. Naat'áanii, p. 25, reel 20, song 2. Naat'áanii commented that the vocables in the chorus represented laughter: "They are happy—everything is put together." Slim Curly's comment in the headnote is from Wyman, p. 115.
16. Naat'áanii, p. 25, reel 20, song 3. It is rare for the phrase "Long-life-returning" to be used without the accompanying phrase "Causing-

happiness-everywhere." No explanation was obtained.

17. Naat'áanii, p. 25, reel 20, song 4.
18. Naat'áanii, p. 26, reel 20, song 5.
19. Naat'áanii, p. 26, reel 21, song 1.
20. Naat'áanii, p. 26, reel 21, song 3. In Wyman, pp. 118–119, and Frisbie (1967), pp. 130–131, Slim Curly and Frank Mitchell both indicated that the vocables in the chorus of this song included the call of Talking God.
21. Naat'áanii, pp. 26–27, reel 22, song 2.
22. Wyman, pp. 140–141.
23. Wyman, p. 176.
24. Mitchell, Frank, *Blessingway Texts*, pp. 1–2, reel 1, song 1, recorded by David P. McAllester, 1957. The tapes are deposited in the Archives of World Music, Wesleyan University. See also Wyman, pp. 177–178, and Frisbie (1967), pp. 168–209, for other versions of this and for subsequent Talking God House songs.
25. Mitchell, p. 3, reel 1, song 4.
26. Mitchell, p. 3, reel 1, song 7.
27. Curly, River Junction, *Blessingway Texts*, pp. 311–312, recorded by Fr. Berard Haile, between 1929 and 1932. Fr. Berard's translation is in Wyman, pp. 539–540. I have retranslated according to the principles stated on pp. 16–17. The phrase "Danger-all-around" is an indication of the Enemyway element referred to by Wyman (p. xxiii).
28. Smith, James, *Enemy Blessingway Texts*, pp. 1–2, reel 2, song 9, recorded by David P. McAllester, 1957. The tapes are deposited in the Archives of World Music, Wesleyan University. Here, as in the preceding song, there is the mixture of Enemyway with Blessingway. James Smith made this explicit in the name by which he identified the material.

29. Hastiin Tł'a'í, *Creation Chant Texts*, pp. 301–304, cylinder 191, song 51a. My retranslation.
30. Winnie, Ray, *Shootingway Texts*, p. 55, reel 4, song 113, recorded by David P. McAllester, 1958. The tapes are deposited in the Archives of World Music, Wesleyan University.
31. Wyman, p. 632.
32. Curly, Slim, *Blessingway Texts*, pp. 248–250, recorded by Fr. Berard Haile in 1932. I have expanded Fr. Berard's condensed notes and added some of the vocables on the model of other songs in this set. This is a fuller version than my earlier translation in Wyman, p. 189.
33. Wyman, pp. 219–220.
34. Wyman, p. 234.
35. Curly, Slim, *Blessingway Texts*, pp. 473–481, song 16 in a set of 37. I have followed the principles stated on pp. 16–17 in my translation. Fr. Berard's own translation is in Wyman, pp. 276–281. For a discussion of this list as representing treasured property in early Navajo culture, and for the force of "my child" as a petition for ownership, see Wyman, p. 276, notes 198 and 199. My own thought is that "its child," which I also find in the Navajo text, suggests the essence of these gifts rather than any particular coyote robe, etc., thus conveying a continual likelihood, over one's lifetime, of receiving such gifts.

SELECTED BIBLIOGRAPHY

Adair, John. *The Navajo and Pueblo Silversmiths.* University of Oklahoma Press, Norman, Oklahoma, 1944. Beautifully illustrated historical account.

Coolidge, Dane, and Mary Roberts Coolidge. *The Navajo Indians.* Houghton Mifflin Company, Boston and New York, 1930. An early, useful account of many aspects of Navajo life.

Dyk, Walter. *Son of Old Man Hat.* Harcourt, Brace and Co., New York, 1938. The life of a Navajo in his own words from childhood to early manhood. A superb narration of everyday Navajo life when outside contacts were still rare.

Frisbie, Charlotte J. *Kinaaldá: A Study of the Navaho Girl's Puberty Ceremony.* Wesleyan University Press, Middletown, Connecticut, 1967. The only detailed study of this aspect of Blessingway; song texts and music include many house songs.

Frisbie, Charlotte J., and David P. McAllester, eds. *Navajo Blessingway Singer: The Autobiography of Frank Mitchell, 1881–1967.* University of Arizona Press, Tucson, 1978. Contains description of Blessingway, myth, song texts, much ethnohistorical material.

Gilpin, Laura. *The Enduring Navaho.* University of Texas Press, Austin, 1968. Beautiful photographs from 1930's to mid-1960's showing many aspects of Navajo life, both traditional and new.

Haile, Father Berard. "Some Cultural Aspects of the Navajo Hogan." Fort Wingate, Arizona, 1937. (Mimeographed.) A brief (7-page) discussion, but with much information on structure and religious associations of the hogan. Two abbreviated house song texts.

Kluckhohn, Clyde, and Dorothea Leighton. *The Navaho,* revised edition. Harvard University Press, Cambridge, Massachusetts, 1974. This is still the standard general book, though it is essentially unchanged from the original edition of 1946.

Moon, Sheila. *A Magic Dwells: A Poetic and Psychological Study of the Navaho Emergence Myth.* Wesleyan University Press, Middletown, Connecticut, 1970. A Jungian discussion of human nature as seen in the myth, perceptive and imaginative.

McCombe, Leonard, Evon Z. Vogt, and Clyde Kluckhohn. *Navaho Means People.* Harvard University Press, Cambridge, Massachusetts, 1951. The best photo-essay on Navajo life in the early 1950's: from misery in the slums to everyday and ceremonial scenes on the reservation.

Reichard, Gladys A. *Navajo Religion: A Study of Symbolism.* Pantheon Books, New York, 1950. A 743-page monument to a lifetime of sensitive research. General discussion and three concordances.

Spencer, Katherine. *Reflections of Social Life in the Navaho Origin Myth.* University of New Mexico Publications in Anthropology no. 3, Albuquerque, 1947. All Navajo myths recorded up to 1947 are summarized and given anthropological and psychological discussion.

Underhill, Ruth M. *The Navajos.* University of Oklahoma Press, Norman, Oklahoma, 1956. (Third printing, 1963). The best history of the Navajo people, based on archaeological, ethnographic, and oral-history evidence.

Wheelwright, Mary C. *Navajo Creation Myth.* Museum of Navajo Ceremonial Art, Santa Fe, New Mexico, 1942. Elements of myths from many different ceremonies are combined here for their relevance to the creation story. A number of sandpaintings and song texts are presented, including a hogan song.

Witherspoon, Gary. *Language and Art in the Navajo Universe.* University of Michigan Press, Ann Arbor, 1977. Very perceptive discussion of Navajo philosophy and its expression in language and the arts.

Wyman, Leland C. *Blessingway.* University of Arizona Press, Tucson, Arizona, 1970. Fr. Berard Haile's 1,850 pages of typescript containing three versions of the Blessingway myth are meticulously edited, with much reference to over two thousand pages of original holograph recordings. Hundreds of song and prayer texts are presented.

LIST OF PHOTOGRAPHS

Mountain-around-which-traveling-was-done (Huerfano Mesa) was the site
of Changing Woman's first home of her own. The hexagonal or octagonal
cribbed-roof hogan still much in use on the Navajo Reservation is said
to take its shape from that of the mesa.   Title spread

HOGANS : Navajo Houses and House Songs

has been composed in Century Expanded by Kingsport Press
and P & M Typesetting, and printed on S. D. Warren's
Lustro Offset Enamel Dull by the Meriden Gravure Company.
Binding by Robert Burlen & Son. Editorial supervision:
Joan Bothell; design: Jorgen G. Hansen and Willard A. Lockwood;
expediters: Eleanor Bloch and Barbara Ras.

WESLEYAN UNIVERSITY PRESS
Middletown, Connecticut
1980